T0384331

THE BOOK OF THE BOSS

POP PRESS

2

Pop Press, an imprint of Ebury Publishing
20 Vauxhall Bridge Road
London SW1V 2SA

Pop Press is part of the Penguin Random House group of companies
whose addresses can be found at global.penguinrandomhouse.com

Penguin
Random House
UK

Copyright © Pop Press 2024
Illustrations Ollie Mann
Page design Ed Pickford
Text Becky Alexander

Flag pattern used on page iv and throughout, adapted from
'Set of nine american flags with variety of designs' designed by
Freepik. star shape used on page 1 and throughout, adapted
from Vintage star icons designed by milano83 on Freepik.

First published by Pop Press in 2024

www.penguin.co.uk

A CIP catalogue record for this book is available from the British Library

ISBN: 9781529933369

Typeset in 10/14.3 pt ITC Franklin Gothic LT Pro by Jouve (UK), Milton Keynes
Printed and bound in Great Britain by Clays Ltd, Elcograf S.p.A.

The authorised representative in the EEA is Penguin Random House
Ireland, Morrison Chambers, 32 Nassau Street, Dublin D02 YH68

MIX
Paper | Supporting
responsible forestry
FSC® C018179

Penguin Random House is committed to a
sustainable future for our business, our readers
and our planet. This book is made from Forest
Stewardship Council® certified paper.

CONTENTS

INTRODUCTION

Throw on your best denim jacket baby, grab your guitar, and buckle up for these wise words from The Boss. Don't just stand there, dancing in the dark – learn how to live your best glory days!

From humble beginnings in New Jersey, to becoming one of the world's most successful and beloved artists, Bruce has lived through a *lot*.

Whether you are born in the USA or not, this book has something for you. Champion of the working-class man, but also friends with presidents, Bruce speaks to all of us.

Songwriter, poet and political activist, Bruce has spoken up for military veterans, racial equality and gay rights. Bruce probably even influenced the fall of the Berlin Wall, following his rallying words at a concert in the city. He has shared his own experience of depression, and is a figure-head for strength, resilience, family life and friendship.

Loved around the world, Bruce has sold millions of albums and won countless awards, including an Oscar for best song ('Streets of Philadelphia'). Known for his marathon 4-hour concerts, his fans love his concerts and performances – he is famously energetic for a man in his 70s! All together now – Brooooooce!

If you are looking for the promised land, or feel like a wreck on the highway, Bruce can tell you how to rise up. Tramps like us, honey, we were born to read this book.

MUSIC

'Man, when I was nine
I couldn't imagine
anyone not wanting to
be Elvis Presley.'

'You can change a life
in three minutes with
the right song.'

'I went into
rock 'n' roll music
to create order out
of my life.'

'A good song takes on
more meaning as the
years pass by.'

'That's the life, the gun-slinging life.'

'The release date is ephemeral. The record is forever.'

'Music saved me.'

'The best music is essentially there to provide you something to face the world with.'

'There is a real patriotism underneath the best of my music but it is a critical, questioning and often angry patriotism.'

'[Mountain of Love] has some of the best lines, and some of the dumbest.'

CREATIVITY

'You're always writing about yourself . . . you hide it in a variety of ways.'

'I try to tell the story
I've been in the
process of telling for
a long time.'

'I used to write every day, on the buses, on the streets . . .'

'To me a song is a vision, a flash.'

'The songwriter always gets another shot to get it right.'

'I wait for the songs
to come along.'

'In my songs, the spiritual part, the hope part, is in the choruses.'

'You're the storyteller. You're the magician.'

FRIENDSHIP

'I've gotten to work
with the people I love
the most.'

'You don't make that many friendships later in life.' [on his friendship with Barack Obama]

'Those are my guys, greatest band I've ever played with.'
[on the E Street Band]

'I am going to throw
the wildest party
you've ever seen. And
you, my friends, are
all invited.'

'Where you come from is like your family and your best friend.'

'Imagine this people. You're going to high school right now, when you're 70 years old, those are the exact people you'll be working with.'

'I enjoyed the camaraderie of being in a band, even though its filled with the usual tension and ebb and flow of life, you know.'

'It's just one of the deepest experiences of my life. I love all of you beyond words.'

LOVE AND FAMILY

'Family life . . . really
is the ultimate
enrichment of the
time we spend here.'

'You take it a day at a time and hope everything works out.' [on marriage]

'As a parent you're trying to guide them along their own path.'

'Those that pass
away, never really
leave us.'

'Pain slips away, the love remains.'

'She was stable enough and strong enough and she brought a lot of love, so those were very healing things over a long period of time.' [on his wife, Patti Scialfa]

'No child wants to see 50,000 people cheer their parents.'

'My secret weapon.' [on Patti Scialfa]

'We're always trying
to find somebody
whose broken pieces
fit with our broken
pieces.'

POLITICS

'Some things are more important than a rock show and this fight against prejudice and bigotry [· · ·] is one of them.'

'Anybody can say anything.'

'I have spent my life judging the distance between American reality and the American dream.'

'Blind faith in your leaders, or in anything, will get you killed.'

'The American idea is a beautiful idea. It needs to be preserved, served, protected and sung out.'

'You can't have a United States if you are telling some folks that they can't get on the train.'

'It's just a game of shadows and mirrors.'

'I do sometimes wonder who went in my place [to the Vietnam war], because somebody did.'

'I was a stone-cold
draft dodger.'

[On performing in East Berlin before the fall of the Berlin Wall] 'I've come to play rock 'n' roll for you in the hope that one day all the barriers will be torn down.'

SUCCESS

'The deepest
motivation comes out
of the house that I
grew up in.'

'We wanted to play because we wanted to meet girls, make a ton of dough and change the world.'

'Success makes life easier. It doesn't make living easier.'

'The next moment holds no guarantees.'

'Having a building
with your name on it
is a tricky thing,
because I'm still
alive.'

'I think you have to make a point of behaving like a human being.'

'I live high on the hog.'

'It's a job that's filled with ego and vanity and narcissism, and you need all those things to do it well.'

'My greatest fear was that success was going to change or diminish that part of myself.'

'If you're good, you're always looking over your shoulder.'

PERFORMING

'When the metal hits
the pedal – bang!'

'Those are my guys,
greatest band I've
ever played with.'

'You put it out there and people hear it, and then it's up to them.'

'I wanted it to sound enormous, to grab you by your throat and insist that you take that ride.'

'My show is just me, the guitar, the piano and the words and music.'

'You want the earth to shake and spit fire!'

'That ticket is me promising you that it's gonna be all the way every chance I get.'

'I can bring this,
this happiness,
these smiles.'

'I never did a lot of drugs, never drank to extreme, I never stayed up after shows and talked all night long, or partied all night long.'

'If there's any complaints on the way out, you can have your money back.'

CONFIDENCE

'The first day I can remember looking into a mirror and being able to stand what I saw was the day I had a guitar in my hand.'

'You've got to make
your own map.'

'All you needed to do was to risk being your true self.'

'You have to be willing to roll the dice.'

'You can't afford
despair, you gotta
find faith someplace.'

'All I know is this –
it's all gonna work
out, one way or
another.'

'There's no ceiling here.'

'I bumped into the luckiest job in the world, because they gave me a fortune for something I would've done for free.'

'I feel like I'm on the outside of all this, even though I know I'm on the inside.'

STANDING UP
FOR OTHERS

'It's no good if it's just for one, it's gotta be for everyone.'

'There's a lot of stuff
being taken away
from a lot of people
that shouldn't have it
taken away from.'

'We are the new American resistance.'

'We're here to testify to what we have seen.'

'When you're putting yourself into shoes you haven't worn, you have to be very thoughtful.'

'I've long believed in and have always spoken out for the rights of same sex couples.'

'I don't think the American dream was that everyone was going to make . . . a billion dollars . . . it was that everyone was going to have . . . the chance to live a life with some decency and . . . self-respect.'

'There's a lot of fire in the burning, but it don't do you any good if you ain't got the hammer for the building.'

'I'm the hope guy.'

'People should come
before profit, and the
community before
the corporation.'

GETTING OLDER

'One's coming of age
has to be earned.'

'You are a raindrop.'

'I'm old. I take a lot of things in my stride.'

'The bill collector is knocking, and his payment'll be in tears.'

'As you get older, the price you pay for not sorting through your [emotional] baggage increases.'

'You can't be afraid of getting old. Old is good, if you're gathering in life.'

'I found that as you get older you accrue a certain sort of richness in your abilities and it's fun to explore that.'

'The song transcends your age.'

'That's just life, and it all goes on without you.'

ACKNOWLEDGEMENTS

Page 8 from Time Magazine, 'The Backstreet Phantom of Rock' (James Willwerth, 1975). Page 9 from The Guardian, 'You can change a life in three minutes with the right song.' (Michael Hann, 2016). Page 10 from The Guardian, 'You can change a life in three minutes with the right song.' (Michael Hann, 2016). Page 11 from The Guardian, 'Bruce Springsteen says years of depression left him crushed' (Nadia Khomami, 2016). Page 12 from NPR, 'Ed Norton interviews Bruce Springsteen on 'Darkness', Toronto Film Festival (2010). Page 13 from The Observer, 'How Bruce Springsteen made Born to Run an American Masterpiece' (Peter Gerstenzang, 2015). Page 14 from Time Magazine, 'The Backstreet Phantom of Rock' (James Willwerth, 1975). Page 15 from The Guardian, 'The Boss Picks His Voice of America' (Andrew Anthony, 2008). Page 16 from The Guardian, 'What was done to my country was un-American' (Fiachra Gibbons, 2012). Page 17 from The Quietus, 'How Born To Run Saved The Boss' (Dave Marsh, 1975). Page 20 from NPR, 'Morning Edition Interview' (Renee Montagne, 2005). Page 21 from Vox, 'Talking to the Boss' (Adam Sweeting, 1992). Page 22 from Sounds, 'Bruce Springsteen' (Jerry Gilbert, 1974). Page 23 from Sounds, 'Bruce Springsteen' (Jerry Gilbert, 1974). Page 24 from NPR, 'Morning Edition: What Does Born in The USA Really Mean' (Steve Inskeep, Barry Gordemer, Vince Pearson, 2019). Page 25 from Variety, 'Bruce Springsteen talks catalog sale' (Michele Amabile Angermiller, 2022). Page 26 from NPR, 'Morning Edition: What Does Born in The USA Really Mean' (Steve Inskeep, Barry Gordemer, Vince Pearson, 2019). Page 27 from CBS News, '60 Minutes'

(John Hamlin, 2007). Page 30 from CBS News, 'Gayle King Interview' (2019). Page 31 from BBC, 'The Graham Norton Show' (2021). Page 32 from Rolling Stone, 'Bruce Springsteen responds to fan outrage over ticket prices' (Andy Greene, 2022). Page 33 from AARP The Magazine, 'Bruce Springsteen Shares About Love, Loss, Aging and the Challenges of Writing his New Album' (Bob Love, 2020). Page 34 from Uncut, 'I Think I Just Wanted to be Great' (Adam Sweeting, 2002). Page 35 from CBS, 'The Late Show with Stephen Colbert' (2020). Page 36 from CBS, 'The Late Show with Stephen Colbert' (2020). From Letter to You (Dir. Thom Zimny, 2020). Page 40 from 'The Bellissimo Files, 'Bruce Springsteen talks about being the boss' (2019). Page 41 from 'The Bellissimo Files, 'Bruce Springsteen talks about being the boss' (2019). Page 42 from CBS News, 'Gayle King Interview' (2019). Page 43 from Apple Music, Zane Lowe Interview (2020). Page 44 from Apple Music, Zane Lowe Interview (2020). Page 45 from Daily Mail, 'She Bought a Lot of Love' (Chloe-Lee Longhetti, 2016). Page 46 from Late Night with Seth Meyers (2022). Page 47 from NME, 'Bruce Springsteen inducts wife and bandmate into New Jersey hall of fame' (Scott Ng, 2023). Page 46 from Western Stars (dir. Thom Zimny, 2019). Page 52 from brucespringsteen.net, 'A statement from Bruce Springsteen on North Carolina' (2016). Page 53 from Uncut, 'I Think I Just Wanted to be Great' (Adam Sweeting, 2002). Page 54 from The Guardian, 'What was done to my country was un-American' (Fiachra Gibbons, 2012). Page 55 from The Guardian, 'The Boss Picks His Voice of America' (Andrew Anthony, 2008). Page 56 from CBS News, '60 Minutes' (John Hamlin, 2007). Page 57 from The Guardian, 'What was done to my country was un-American' (Fiachra Gibbons, 2012). Page 58 from Entertainment Weekly, 'Springsteen Talks' (Ken Tucker, 2003). Page 59 from Springsteen on Broadway (Dir. Thom Zimny, 2018). Page 60 from Tribeca Talks: Storytellers with Bruce Springsteen and Tom Hanks (2017). Page 61 from Spiegel International, 'How Springsteen Helped Tear Down the Wall' (David Crossland, 2013).

ACKNOWLEDGEMENTS

Page 64 from CNN, 'Bruce Springsteen and the song of the working man' (Todd Leopold, 2012). Page 65 from Rolling Stone, 'Bruce Springsteen on 'Born in the USA'' (Kurt Loder, 1984). Page 66 from Q Magazine, 'Bruce Springsteen' (David Hepworth, 1992). Page 67 from Born to Run, Bruce Springsteen (2016). Page 68 from Variety, 'Bruce Springsteen to have building named after him at Jersey Monmouth University' (Michele Amabile Angermiller, 2023). Page 69 from Uncut, 'I Think I Just Wanted to be Great' (Adam Sweeting, 2002). Page 70 from The New Yorker, 'We Are Alive' (David Remnick, 2012). Page 71 from The New Yorker, 'We Are Alive' (David Remnick, 2012). Page 72 from The Guardian, 'People thought we were gone. Finished.' (Keith Cameron, 2010). Page 73 from NPR, 'Ed Norton interviews Bruce Springsteen on 'Darkness', Toronto Film Festival (2010). Page 76 from Time Magazine, 'Bruce Rising' (Josh Tyrangiel & Kate Carcaterra, 2002). Page 77 from Rolling Stone, 'Bruce Springsteen responds to fan outrage over ticket prices' (Andy Greene, 2022). Page 78 from CNN, 'Bruce Springsteen and the song of the working man' (Todd Leopold, 2012). Page 79 from Rolling Stone, 'Bruce Springsteen's Born to Run turns 30' (Brian Hiatt, 2005). Page 80 from The New York Times, 'Bruce Springsteen is bringing his music and memories to Broadway' (2017). Page 81 from Wall Street Journal, 'Springsteen looks back on 'Born to Run'' (Ashley Kahn, 2005). Page 82 from The Star, 'Bruce Springsteen: Can his shows be too long?' (Ben Rayner, 2012). Page 83 from Rolling Stone, 'Bruce Springsteen's Enthralling New Memoir' (Andy Greene, 2016). Page 84 from USA Today, 'Bruce Springsteen talks singing soul and 'clean living'' (Chris Jordan, 2022). Page 85 from Rolling Stone, 'Bruce Springsteen responds to fan outrage over ticket prices' (Andy Greene, 2022). Page 88 from Esquire, 'Springsteen's long long overdue guitar album' (Ryan D'Agostino, 2014). Page 89 from Rolling Stone, 'Bruce Springsteen: The Rolling Stone Interview' (Joe Levy, 2007). Page 90 from Esquire, 'Beneath the surface of Bruce Springsteen' (Michael Hainey, 2018). Page 91 from

Entertainment Weekly, "Springsteen Talks' (Ken Tucker, 2003). Page 92 from Vox, 'Talking to The Boss' (Adam Sweeting, 1992). Page 93 from Rolling Stone, 'Bringing it all back home' (David Fricke, 2009). Page 94 from Billboard, The Billboard Cover Q&A, (Ray Waddell, 2009). Page 95 from Variety, 'Bruce Springsteen talks catalog sale' (Michele Amabile Angermiller, 2022). Page 96 from Time Magazine, 'The Backstreet Phantom of Rock' (James Willwerth, 1975). Page 100 from Politico Magazine, 'How Ronald Reagan changed Bruce Springsteen's Politics' (Marc Dolan,2014). Page 101 from Politico Magazine, 'How Ronald Reagan changed Bruce Springsteen's Politics' (Marc Dolan,2014). Page 102 from Rolling Stone, 'Bruce Springsteen on Women's March' (Daniel Kreps, 2017). Page 103 from Time Magazine, 'Bruce Rising' (Josh Tyrangiel & Kate Carcaterra, 2002). Page 104 from Time Magazine, 'Bruce Rising' (Josh Tyrangiel & Kate Carcaterra, 2002). Page 105 from Billboard, 'Bruce Springsteen Speaks Out For Gay Marriage, (Monica Herrera, 2009). Page 106 from The Atlantic, 'Born to Run and the decline of the American dream' (Joshua Zeitz, 2015). Page 107 from Rolling Stone, 'Bruce Springsteen: The Rolling Stone Interview' (Joe Levy, 2007). Page 108 from Renegades: Born in the USA Podcast (2021). Page 109 from Rolling Stone, 'Bruce Springsteen on 'Born in the USA" (Kurt Loder, 1984). Page 112 from Esquire, 'Beneath the surface of Bruce Springsteen' (Michael Hainey, 2018). Page 113 from The New Yorker, 'We Are Alive' (David Remnick, 2012). Page 114 from Rolling Stone, 'Bruce Springsteen responds to fan outrage over ticket prices' (Andy Greene, 2022). Page 115 from Esquire, 'Beneath the surface of Bruce Springsteen' (Michael Hainey, 2018). Page 116 from Entertainment Weekly, 'Springsteen Talks' (Ken Tucker, 2003). Page 117 from The Guardian, 'People thought we were gone. Finished.' (Keith Cameron, 2010). Page 118 from USA Today, 'Bruce Springsteen talks singing soul and 'clean living" (Chris Jordan, 2022). Page 119 from Rolling Stone, 'Bruce Springsteen's Born to Run turns 30' (Brian Hiatt, 2005). Page 120 from Rolling Stone, 'Bringing it all back home' (David Fricke, 2009).